The Coming DIVINE Accounting

By Dawn Densmore-Parent

Dedication

"To the LORD Jesus Christ and to Family and Friends!"

Many Thanks!
dawn

Cover Design

Tamara Smith, UVM Print and Mail, VT

© Copyright 2025

ISBN

978-1-7342353-7-1

INTRODUCTION

This book is a compilation of true events that occurred during my 70+ years on earth. With the bulk of those years now behind me, the eternal promises in the Bible have **significantly** more interest. Most of my life has required that I plug into each day with my 'heart'. We must exercise 'faith" when we do not 'understand" to be able get thru life's challenging times! It is faith in what is 'not' seen, that empowers us to *pray* in the middle of it all, and to trust God to work what is seen as 'bad' for our 'good'.

It is my deepest desire that these true accounts will inspire you to also seek God's will each day in your life, and then *'get up and do your very best'*; because doing 'that' is what is well pleasing in God's sight!

Looking back, it is the 'bad' things that made me kneel and ask God for His help, and this is exactly where living an extraordinarily miraculous life begins! We are told to: **ASK – SEEK – KNOCK!**

"Trust in the Lord with all thine heart

and lean NOT unto thine own understanding.

In all thine ways acknowledge Him

and He shall direct thy path!" Proverbs 3:5-6

Dawn Densmore- Parent

Dawn Densmore-Parent

Chapter 1 – My Early Years 7

Chapter 2 – The Search 15

Chapter 3 – Unexpected Answers 19

Chapter 4 – The Supernatural Reality 23

Chapter 5 – The Unexpected 27

Chapter 6 – Confirmation: God IS in Charge! 35

Chapter 7 – Visitations from Above 39

Chapter 8 – The Outing 41

Chapter 9 – Courage in Action 43

Chapter 10 – Unexpected Blessings 45

Chapter 11 – The Divine Meeting 47

Chapter 12 – God's Divine Answers 51

Chapter 13 – The Divine Assignment 55

Chapter 14 – Yielded to Divine Guidance 59

Chapter 15 - Yielded 65

Chapter 16 –The Supernatural 69

Chapter 17 –Be Prepared 75

Chapter 18 – The Coming DIVINE Accounting 81

Chapter 19 – The "Dash" 87

Chapter 20 - The Biblical Record 93

Dawn Densmore-Parent

Chapter 1 – My Early Years

All that I am going to tell you, literally happened! My life has been quite a bit like the 'feather' that was moved by the 'wind' featured in the movie "Forrest Gump" bringing with it spontaneous different events. But my 'life' rather than being like a 'box of chocolates', has been like 'flowers in a field with manure' which requires one who goes to pick those flowers, to step carefully with your feet to avoid coming out very 'stinky!

Each step provided a divine opportunity to return 'love' for 'hate'! And like Forrest Gump's mom's view, the Lord truly does have a very special plan for each and every person. In fact, God wants us to become like His 'little children'.

God made us to "choose to love Him" and to "care and love one another". That requires us to be willing to make 'sacrifices'.

Often it is our police officers and fireman who arrive, trained and ready to risk their lives, to help us when things go wrong. I witnessed a lot of that! I married a man who became a police officer. He almost died twice from being assaulted while on duty, and he actually was instrumental in saving a young boy's life.

Unlike Forrest Gump, I never had a child of my own, but very much like Forrest Gump, I went with what life handed me. Forrest Gump had friends to help him, and so did I. And like Forrest Gump, who married his childhood sweetheart, I, too, would end up marrying the boy that I had a crush on in high school, but before that would happen, I would end up marrying Jim who became a police officer. Jim and I had 23 wonderful years together, but sadly, my remembrance of a buried unexpected event would cause both us to agree to live separately; and then to agree to divorce. We remain friends.

Growing Up

In my 'day' there were BIG farm families! I was one of 9 children. There were 8 girls and 1 boy. I was the 4th one down. I was designated as a "black sheep", partly because I liked to dress up in white, and also because I loved to play with dolls. I was tagged as 'city people'. My sisters were "Tom boys" out exploring 'fun' new things to do! I was not interested in putting on 'mud stockings or mud gloves' made from the 'mud' in our brook by our cows as they came in and out of that brook, or in looking for 'salamanders' in the brook in the woods, catching frogs, insects, or butterfly hunting with nets in ditches. These were some of the things that I wanted nothing to do with!

I loved to take my baby doll in her baby carriage and push her up and down our long driveway to the barn and back to the house. I was picked on for doing this, and that would result in my hearing God's voice speak to me for the very first –but NOT the last time!

My Life Saver

When I was very young, I found a lifesaver and put it in my mouth. Then, I coughed, and that lifesaver got wedged inside my throat. I could not breathe or speak, and was gasping for air and turning red. My Grandma saw me and immediately came and picked me by my ankles and pulled me upside down and shook me up and down several times. When nothing came out, she continued to hold me upside down with one hand and used her other hand to slap my back very hard, and as she did that, out popped that Lifesaver onto the floor! My Grammy saved my life from a "lifesaver" that day!
Grammy and Grandpa lived on the first floor of our farmhouse. That was the only time she slapped my back, but she also spanked my bottom several times!

The Mysterious Bureau
As a toddler my favorite thing was to pull out the lower drawer of a bedroom bureau. I had to work hard to get the drawer open, but once opened, I proceeded to pull everything out, tossing things on the floor behind me. I wanted to crawl into the open space at the back of that drawer. At first, Grammy just scolded me and would pick me up and move me and then put everything back that I had worked so hard to remove! Eventually she would spank my bottom! She asked, "Why are you doing this?! You need to stop doing this!" I could not talk, but I wanted to show her that I had found a special opening to go into. That Bureau, to me, was like the C.S. Lewis bureau that miraculously opened to another dimension.

My Questions

That bureau drawer seemed to have potential answers to my questions. Very early in my life I wanted to know what 'life' was all about! Why were we here? Why did people have to die? There seemed to be no answers to my questions.

When I got older, I was so frustrated I almost took my own life, but the Lord helped me to decide to "just wait and get some sleep!" I thought, "I can 'after all' do that in the morning --if I still want to." But I had a dream and when I awoke, I was very glad that I had not taken an overdose of pills that could have ended my life.

And it would be another dream of me being 'dead' and yet 'alive' and of finding myself in a huge space in another dimension where I would recall all of the events in my life that I had kept secret. In the dream, there were a lot of others waiting to give their 'account.' As I waited for my turn for my life's 'accounting', I had time to remember all the 'secrets' that I knew 'now' would be revealed!

Here, people would ask me, "Why didn't you tell me these things?" And I knew I would say, "Because I was afraid of what you would think of me!" Then suddenly, I was 'awake' and laying in my bed. I immediately got out of my bed and got on my knees on the floor. The dream had been so very real! Tears fell from my eyes. I thanked the Lord that I was back in 'my body' and that I had time to do better!

My Very First Secret

My first secret was of actually hearing God's voice speak directly to me using my name! It involved my trying to play with my doll and my doll carriage. I had been threatened by one of my older sisters, "You keep pushing that stroller with your doll, and I will take that baby and toss her on the ground and stomp on her!"

This made me very afraid, so I started using just the lower part of our driveway where no one could see me to push my baby stroller!
But I got bored with that confined space.

One day I decided to go around the corner and up the driveway with my baby stroller! I had determined to fight to protect my doll! So, around the corner I went! I was ready to fight! But when I got around that corner and looked around, no one was there!

I stood still. I was shocked! I had been afraid of something that was not even there! Suddenly, I heard a voice speak to me: *"Play with your dolls Dawn, you won't always be able to play with your dolls."*
I looked around, to see who had spoken to me! But no one was there! Where did that voice come from? I had no answers. I determined it must be "God"! I was so excited to have the entire driveway, I played as hard as I could that day, pushing my doll carriage up and down the driveway! I was so happy to have heard God speak to me! I knew God was with me! And it would be this one pivotal decision that would provide 'courage' for my life! Whenever I was afraid, I would think of that 'corner' and that voice and I would pray for 'courage' and then I would go forward.

Dawn Densmore-Parent

My First Orange Cat - Ringworm

Our farm had cats that lived in the barn to help control the mouse population. One cat had kittens, and each kitten was designated to belong to one of my sisters. But there were not enough kittens for everyone – we were short by one!

There was an older orange Tom cat that had lost his tail in the motor blade of the milking machine named, "Ringworm". He had a disease called 'ringworm' that you could 'catch' if you touched him, and that is where he got his name.

The day the kittens were claimed, I was told, "You can have Ringworm! Ringworm will be your cat!" Ringworm looked pitiful, but I was not given a choice in the matter.

I felt a lot like 'ringworm' - unloved and rejected! Although I could not touch Ringworm, we became 'buddies'. I would tell him, "Things are going to be alright!"

Many years later, this one event would also provide a divine answered prayer that would encourage me to always pray!

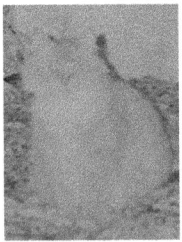

My Miracle Cat – Buffy

The miracle of my cat 'Buffy" would occur after my first husband, Jim and I parted ways. I had begun to date a wonderful man, who I truly wanted to marry. He had two tiger cats and his favorite was "Sebastian". It was a very sad day when Sebastian got ill and passed away. After the loss, I suggested he get another cat, but it was too soon for him to even consider that. But 3 months before Christmas he asked me, "What would you like for Christmas:" I knew he was still missing his cat, so I replied, "I would like a cat! But it will have to be a very special cat in memory of my own first and only cat named "Ringworm". This 'cat' will need to be "**Orange, female, declawed, spayed and free!"**

My friend looked for 3 months but he just could not find any 'cat' that met all of my criteria! He finally told me: "I have nothing for you for Christmas!" Upon this news, I went to an upstairs bedroom and got on my knees and cried and cried. I told the Lord, "I am not crying because I am not getting a cat, I am crying because I have given you my life – all I wanted to know is that I am pleasing in your sight –and finding a cat with those 5 criteria should not be a problem, 'YOU" made cats!"

I then returned downstairs to tell my friend, "It's okay that I get nothing for Christmas, it was not the 'cat' that I wanted anyway! I am truly happy just to have you in my life! "

That next morning was Christmas Eve, and as my friend looked in the free section of the newspaper, he found a posting. That posting said FREE CAT: Buffy, orange, female, declawed, spayed and free". I called the owner on Christmas morning. I was told, "Buffy cannot go to just anyone. I need to meet you before you can have her."

My friend drove me 3 hours to go to meet the owner to see if he would give me Buffy. My friend repeatedly told me to not get my hopes up. But when we arrived and entered the home, Buffy came right up to me! The owner replied, "She has never done THAT before – I guess she IS your cat!"

He then gifted me with all of her food, litter box and toys! My friend and I would endure the 3-hour trip back as Buffy cried all the way home

Once home, Buffy went upstairs to the very bedroom where I had cried and hid under the bed for 3 days. Finally, Buffy came out from under that bed and let me pet her. Buffy was my very special 'cat' because only God can answer such a prayer! Buffy was 'proof' that we ought always to pray and not to faint, for with God all things are possible!

My First Church

As I got older my family allowed me to go to church. We were Catholics and the church was full of high ceilings and stained-glass windows and statutes, but I did not hear any voice from God there. We also went to a Catholic School where I learned about Jesus. In first grade, there was a statue of Jesus as a boy with a red robe and crown on his head. I was told all Catholics went to heaven.

One day on the way to our Catholic church I saw another church and I saw people going into that church. When I asked about those people and that church. I was told, "Those people are not Catholic- and cannot go to heaven" I was alarmed! I wanted to go and tell them, but my concern was ignored.

Chapter 2 – The Search

My Teenage Years

When I was 12, my parents would separate and then divorce. All of us as children remained on the farm with our mom. My father was awarded the lake farm that he had purchased for extra farmland, and my mom received the home farm on Route 7. My Dad would place a trailer on the lake land, and when I was eighteen, I would go between living at the farm with my mom and living with my dad in his trailer.

I did well in High School and was offered a full art scholarship to Boston University, but I did not take it. I could not see how I could support myself with 'art' and I began working as a 'secretary' for the State of Vermont, City of Winooski on a "Model Cities" grant that lasted three years.

During that time, I met Jim and we really liked each other. When the grant ended, I joined my two sisters in Boston and worked for the Shelco Company which was a subsidiary of Clorox for a merchandising manager. I worked hard and when my own job was done, I would use any extra time to help in the Marketing Department where they were creating commercials. I helped with the commercial for 'Tidy Bowl" that had a man in a rowboat – the camera would show the boat in a clear lake and then pan out to reveal that the boat was actually in the back of the toilet bowl tank!

Jim stayed in touch with me and visited me in Boston and it was during a trip to visit me in Boston that he asked me to marry him. When I went to work the next day, I told my boss, "I have something to tell you." He replied, "I also have something to tell you too, but you go first!" I explained that I would be resigning to go back to Vermont to marry the man I had left behind there. He laughed and said, "We are relocating the business to California, and you position is ending. "

My First Marriage

I moved back to Vermont and began work for Equitable Life. Jim was also a Catholic, so we were married at Holy Angels Church on September 29, 1974. Jim and I purchased a rental building with one of his friends. We would eventually purchase a new raised ranch home in Colchester, VT. My deepest desire was to connect with God again. I wanted to understand more about the spiritual meaning of life. So, I started to read every book I could find about the 'occult, magic, and the supernatural realm'. But these books did not have anything about hearing the voice of God. I began to just read the last chapter first, to see what each book was all about and determine if it was worthy of my time!

Three Magic Words

One book that finally got my attention was entitled, "Three Magic Words". What were those 'magic words?' "You are God!" I read the entire book and loved it! This meant that I was in control and could determine my future! As I pondered this, suddenly an 'entity' was upon me attacking me with electricity that went through my body. This was very painful! I was lying on my bed and I cried out, "I am looking for God -who are you?" The entity spoke and said, "You opened the door!" This was NOT what I expected; and I cried out: "God, Help me!"

Then I heard that voice speak to me again, *"Cling to the Cross!"*

So, I envisioned in my mind a cross and as I clung to that 'cross' suddenly, as quickly as 'it' had happened that entity vanished. But I was shaken. "O God, please don't let that happen again!"
"Show me what to do to NOT have that happen again!" Amazingly, I actually had peace in the fact that I had heard God speak to me again.

Jim created a room in our basement with a door for a sewing room where I could work on my new business venture that I called, "Jungle Beasts".

Dawn Densmore-Parent

Chapter 3 – Unexpected Answers

Assurance of Heaven

The next day, Jim asked me to go to the hardware store. Once I arrived, when I went to the isle to get what he requested, an older man stopped me to invite me to a new Bible study that he had started in a school in our town. As he handed me a small invitation card, he asked, "If you died today, do you know if you would go to heaven?" I replied, "Of course, I am a Catholic!" My early church experience had assured me all Catholics go to heaven! He continued, "When did you ask Jesus into your heart?" I replied, "I pray all the time!" He replied, "Are you married?" I replied, "Yes!" He replied, "Well asking Jesus into your heart is like getting married, and you don't do that 'every day'!" He asked, "Do you read the Bible?" I replied, "NO! No one can understand the Bible!" He replied, "Well you have a lot to say about a book you have never read!" What he said, made me think and wonder what the Bible actually said!

My First Bible

I went the very next day and purchased a 'Bible' and started reading "The New Testament". I was amazed that in the Bible there were accounts of people who had heard the voice of God from heaven and also of people attacked by demons! I had no idea any of **"THAT"** was in the Bible! These were just like my own experiences of both, right 'there'! I started attending that bible study in a school classroom. I was excited to learn about the miracles that Jesus performed, as well as the fact that Jesus was able to make demons flee. But one Sunday, I did not like what he said, "Whoever wants to go to heaven needs to repent."

In my mind, 'everyone' belonged to God: therefore no one needed to repent to go to heaven. I determined in my mind that I would leave that day and not go back. I stayed until the end of the bible study.

When I went to exit the school, a man at the door stepped in front of me to block my exiting and said, "I am afraid if you leave here today, you will never come back!" I replied, "That is NOT true!" But it was true! How did HE KNOW!?

My "I Got It!" Moment

I exited that door and continued to walk down the sidewalk to get to my parked car. Suddenly, I heard God speak, *"If you leave now, you are on your own!"* I stopped COLD. Again, I had heard the voice of God! I did not want to do my life alone! I turned around and went back inside the school and walked up to the Minister's wife, Joyce, and said, "I think I need to repent but I don't know what to say?" Joyce asked, "Do you believe that Jesus came, and died and rose again?" I replied, "Yes I do believe that!" Joyce said, "Well, you need to tell him that!" As she said those words, she got on her knees, and I followed her on my knees. I repeated after her words, "Lord, I believe you came and died and rose again!" She said, "Now just ask him to forgive you for your sins!" I thought about my life and the many bad decisions I had made, of the anger I held inside, and said, "Jesus, I am so sorry for the wrong things I have done, please forgive me!" As those words came from my heart out of my mouth, tears gushed from my eyes. I wept as I literally felt the presence of God's Holy Spirit enter into my heart! And I heard God's voice tell me, *"Your life will not be easy, but you will never be alone!"*

Born Again

As I left for the second time that day, instead of feeling angry, I was so happy! I was 'born again' of God's Holy Spirit! I continued to read the Bible and decided to follow Jesus in being fully baptized under water. There was still no church building, so I was baptized in Lake Champlain.

Empowered

I made a new habit to get up early and to take time to start my day with reading from the Bible. Each day I continued to understand more and more. I began to understand and 'know' what the Lord wanted me to do.

One day when I was reading my Bible, I stopped and told God, "If everything in this book is true, then this whole earth is not what it seems to be at all. There is a whole different 'realm' as well as a very different way of living by obeying these words!" Once again, I got on my knees and held up my Bible and said, "Behold the handmaid of the Lord be it done unto me according to thy word – send me!" My husband Jim initially was not interested in going to church with me, but he began to see changes in my disposition and attitude, and he started to go to church with me. He also had a Bible, and he was spending time at night reading the Bible, and soon he too, had prayed and asked God to forgive him and for Jesus to come into his heart.

The Puppets

When I was asked if I wanted to teach a class for children, although I did not feel qualified, I agreed. I designed my own patterns and created stuffed animals, and started making them into puppets with mouths. Jim made me a puppeteer stand with PVC piping that was covered with fabric, and I purchased music to use with the puppets with messages from the Bible.

The older children were given written scripts and used the puppets to do the puppet show for the younger children.

On our back deck on Saturdays, I would invite the children in the neighborhood to come and see a puppet show by my using a blanket over the railing of our back deck.

Our lives were being blessed.

We were stretching out of our comfort zones.

I met new people and made new friends.

One of my new friends was Sue. She lived very close to my home, and we began to chat during the week with one another.

Chapter 4 – The Supernatural Reality

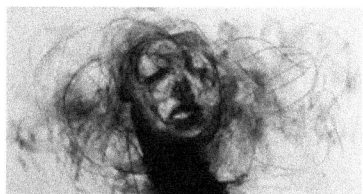

Demon Attack

Jim created a room in our basement with a door for a sewing room where I could work on my new business venture that I called, "Jungle Beasts".

One day when I was in that sewing room, my phone rang, and I went to answer it. Back then, my phone was mounted to the wall next to the door. As I got up from my sewing machine stool and headed to the phone, I watched as the door to the sewing room 'suddenly opened on its own'. I thought how odd! Could I have created enough 'wind' by moving fast to have that happen? That seemed very unlikely.

As I answered the phone and said, "Hello", I heard my new friend Sue say, "Hello" back. But then suddenly I felt a 'demon' jump upon my back and start to push my head and upper body hard into the sewing table. I could not talk and could hardly even breathe. This was just like the first demonic attack, but now my friend Sue heard me gasping for air and asked, "Are you okay?" She started to pray for me over the phone. As she prayed, suddenly the demon left, and I was able to say, "I've been attached by a demon!"

She replied, "I know, it is now here with me!" Then I heard her gasp! She said, "It's now attacking me!" I began praying for her and she said, "It has left me too now!" Both of us were scared, but we both knew God had allowed the attacks. And we also understood that when 'miracles' start to happen, there seems to be an opening as well that allows demons to push back at us.

Walking Tin Man

One year, Sue and I went on a woman's retreat together organized by the Missionary Alliance Church. The church provided its van for the trip to Boston. The retreat had powerful speakers that encouraged us to be vessels for the Lord's use. During this Women's Conference the power of God would forever be clear in my mind as well as evidence of the supernatural currently happening in our world. When the missionary speaker had finished her talk, she gave an invitation to anyone who wanted prayer, to come forward to the church altar. We stood singing from a Hymnal book. I opened the song book to the # given and stood to sing with everyone else. As I stood, I heard the Lord tell me, "Go Forward." I replied, "I don't want to!" Again, the Lord repeated "God Forward." The song was over and I replied, "I will just sit down here." As I sat down, I suddenly felt a swirling energy in my stomach area. The energy now was taking over my entire body, and it lifted me up and got me into the center isle of the church. My hands were still holding the hymn book and were 'locked in place' as my legs moved mechanically up and down as I was 'marched' up to the altar and right up the altar stairs to the missionary who was now seated on the stage. Suddenly the power put me on my knees with the hymnal book landing on her lap. Then the power left me. I looked at the missionary and on her skirt were many 'crowns'.

I said, "Your skirt is full of crowns and the songs on these pages are, 'Crown Him with Many Crowns' and' The King is Coming'!" The missionary said, "I know, thank you." I got up off my knees and went back to my pew seat, but my entire view of life was changed.

I now understood how a person could lift a car all by themselves, and how the Lord could empower 'any one' at 'any time' to accomplish His will, even when we are unwilling participants. I had been like a 'walking tin man' for anyone watching as my legs mechanically were pushed up and down until the 'mission' of the Lord had been accomplished.

Blue Flower Under the Ice

That same missionary would at the end of the week, have one of the people in the church come and hand me an artificial blue flower as I entered the sanctuary. I had no idea 'Why' I had been given a 'blue flower'. Before the conference, I had taken time to make about 30 small gifts that I had given to women that I met during the conference.

Each had a powerful word –

FAITH –

HOPE –

LONGSUFFERING

 GENTLENESS

GOODNESS -

MEEKNESS –

TEMPERANCE –

PATIENCE –

 LOVE, etc.

These words were hand cross-stitched into fabric and put into small frames with magnets on the back to use as fridge magnets. As she finished her final message to all of us, she commented "Experiencing God's love in our world is like finding a blue flower under the ice".

Each of the gift fridge magnets were made with prayer and prayer was made to determine who would get each 'word'. It is when we do what we can with what we have that allows us to connect with something much larger.

This is, in fact, what is missing in our current world that is full of so much yet sadly lacking in producing real joy and peace and love for one another. It is the trials, temptations, and trouble that cause our hearts to be as 'cold' as ice towards God. The presence of the Lord is here with us, and He is able to take something very 'small' to bless those who seek to serve the Lord.

And it is those very trials that soften our heard hearts to be willing to seek the Lord, and when we do that, the Lord is faithful to meet us with His comfort and unconditional love.

Chapter 5 – The Unexpected

The Amazing Ride

The unexplainable events in both of Sue's and my life, made us even closer friends. On the way home from that mission's conference, the church van got to the top of a very steep hill on I-89 headed into Vermont and it stalled. Our driver, Gloria pulled over into the breakdown lane and there we sat in the church van. The van was out of gas! We all began to wonder how long we would be stranded there. There were no cell phones back then!

I was seated in the back of the van and got up to go and speak to Gloria. As I walked to the front of the van, the van started to move ever so slowly. We realized if all of us moved forward together, our combined weight might allow the van to move down the hill. Sure enough! Once we all stood up and went and stood in the front, the van started to move forward, faster and faster it went! Gloria, at first remained in the breakdown lane, but soon she was going 60 mph just like everyone else and moved back into the lane with other traffic.

We knew that the next Exit had a gas station very close to that Exit. I told Gloria, "Don't touch the brakes to slow this down! Keep going and the van may be able to continue to coast slowly right to the gas station!" We encouraged her to put her flashers on and go right through the stop sign! We prayed there would be no car coming, and she was able to go thru that stop sign and pulled the van right up to a gas pump. The question was, "Were we close enough for the gas hose to reach the tank?!"

I was the first one out of the van. As I stretched the gas hose, it just barely reached the tank!. I got down on my knees right there and thanked Jesus for helping us like that! The whole experience was 'bad' but it had turned out 'good'!

The Blackberries

My life was now aligned with a deep desire to be of service to God. We are told we will become His hands, His feet, His eyes, and His ears to the degree we are willing to be available to do so! There would be another miracle that would be a blessing to my friend Sue that would come to her from the Lord through my very own hands.

Jim and I had moved to a new house in Jericho. It was a Saturday morning, when I asked the Lord, "What will you have me to do today? Just let me know and I will do it!" Suddenly, I started thinking about 'blackberries.' I had no idea if there were any blackberries, in this new location, or even if it was blackberry season, but off I went with a pail in hand to see if I could find them. Well, there were 'none'! But as I stopped in front of a bush along a barbed wire fence, I heard the Lord speak to me, "Look under that bush." I thought, "Under the bush?!" I had to get onto my hands and knees but when I looked from the ground under that bush, there were blackberries there! I had to get onto my back to get under that barbed wire fence which was very close to the ground - but I picked and picked – the largest blackberries I had ever seen! I filled my bucket and carefully pushed myself on my back under the fence and walked back home along the road. I thought, "What will I do with all of these blackberries?" Immediately, I thought of my friend Sue. We had not talked in a long time, but when I got home, I called her.

We talked and got caught up on the 'news' and then I said, "I have something that you might like, would you like some blackberries?" She was silent. I said, "You don't have to take them, not everyone likes blackberries, but they're the largest I have ever seen!"

She replied, "That's not it." I asked, "What is it?" Sue replied, "You are not going to believer this, but I told the Lord yesterday I would love some blackberries, but I had no time to go pick them, and if he wanted me to have them, He would have to get them to me! Now, you call this morning and ask me if I want blackberries!" I replied, "O, Sue, I had no idea I would pick blackberries today, I asked the Lord what he would have me to do, and I thought of "Blackberries" and now you tell me this!"

We were both very quiet. God had answered her prayer in a wonderful way, and there was no doubt in our minds of the amazing ways the Lord works to answer our prayers. Some prayers get answered right away but some take years to be answered. But I was learning that those who dedicate their lives to serve God, are privileged to experience the power of God answering our prayers.

The Power of Prayer

My life now began with my reading the bible and getting on my knees in prayer for people in my family and those that were my friends to come to know Jesus too! But it would be an amazing experience that I never asked for or expected that would help me to understand that Jesus is alive in heaven!

The Divine Appearance

One weekend, Jim's brother and wife came to visit, and we gave them our bedroom to sleep in. As Jim and I descended the stairs to our basement to sleep on a sofa bed, my husband grabbed me around the waist and hugged me and said, "There's a full moon tonight!" I had no interest in a full moon, but he was unusually excited about it and repeated, "Yes a full moon and it won't be this full again for a very long time!"

We went to the basement, and I looked out the window, but there was no full moon. We both managed to get to sleep on the sofa bed, and in the night, I felt a nudge on my left side - (but Jim was on my right). I opened my eyes and looked and there was a huge full moon in our basement window. I started to wake Jim but decided not to – and just started telling Jesus that I loved him and wanted to serve him.

Then suddenly the face of a man appeared – I waved and said, "Hi Jesus!" and then realized how silly it was –I could NOT be seeing Jesus! I told the Lord I was 'crazy' and said, "I am going to close my eyes and when I open them if you are still there, I will know I am seeing you!" But when I opened my eyes 'He was gone' and I was 'relieved' and continued to thank and praise him. But then there he appeared again. and the 2ND time he had a ½ smile on his face and then he disappeared.

The next day, my husband and I rode together as I dropped him off at the police station. He said, "What is going on, you are very quiet" I replied, "Well I wasn't going to tell you, but I saw Jesus's face in the moon last night!" There was silence.

"I repeated, "I know it sounds crazy, but I saw him not once but twice!" As he got out of the car, and I walked around to the driver's seat, he said, "We can talk about this later!" But we never did talk about 'it'. This would be another 'secret' that I would keep to myself – for fear of what others would think of me.

The Confirmation

The morning of that appearance was June 28, 1980. My Bible reading that day was in John, Chapter 14, and when I came to verse 21, I froze. It reads, *"He that hath my commandments, and keepnet them, he it is that loveth me, and he that loveth me shall be loved of my Father, and I will love him and will __manifest__ myself to him."*

A Repeat Experience

It would be 42 years later, June 24, 2022, when I would be rereading my book, *"For Such a Time as This?"*.

I had gifted this book to our friends after COVID, and I felt the Lord wanted me to read it again. So after I had dropped the book off, I returned home and sat on our couch to read it.

Fabien, my 2nd husband, was working outside when I got home. Then while reading the verses at the end of that book about the days of Noah and being ready for the 'rapture.'. Fabien came to our back door and insisted that I come to see something. I put the book down on the couch and went with him. I thought he wanted to show me an animal or a home of an animal!

But NO, he wanted me to see the full moon that was over the lake appearing in the water – it was the very same image of the cover of the book I was re-reading.

I said, "You know what book I was reading when you came to get me? "The same book, *"For Such a Time as This?"* that has this image of the moon on the water on the cover!"

Fabien exclaimed, "No way!"

I replied, "Yes and I was reading about the 'rapture" when you came to get me!"

This was almost the exact repeat of 1980 experience with my first husband Jim, who had been so excited about a full moon, and both moons were 'strawberry moons' – that only occur once in a great while. So, we know Jesus is coming again for His own -as we are now seeing the' signs in the moon' of that return in the air for us.

Face to Face with Death

I would have another amazing miracle that would save me from a car accident, assuring me of God's control in an amazing way!

My mom was having memory issues, and was put into a nursing home and I went to visit her –she could only talk now in French and I did not know French –so visiting was a challenge.

One week, I was asked to go for a special occasion at the nursing home, and left after work. I wanted to go and come home as quick as I could, so I pressed on the gas pedal to speed up as I went. I heard a voice say, "Slow down" - I took my foot off the gas pedal and pushed in a cassette tape and looked up to see a car in my lane, passing 2 other cars on a hill.

The driver of that car was young and was going 80-100+ mph!

I thought 'this is it' but as he turned the wheel hard to the right, his car went sideways across the road, missing my car and the 2nd car he was passing by less than an inch each.

I watched as he pulled the wheel hard to the left and his car went into the ditch and then right back onto the road.

I looked at the face of the driver of that first car that I met, in disbelief, then at the face of the second car driver in disbelief! I drove over the hill, and I pulled my car off the road and parked it on the side of the road.

My hands were frozen to the wheel.

My knees were knocking together.

We had almost had a 4-car pile-up.

But I knew something the other three drivers did not know!

Had I not heard the voice, "Slow down!" and had I not immediately removed my foot from off the gas – there would NOT have been those extra 'seconds' for that young driver to navigate through 'right to left' across the road with his car, and likely his great speed would have caused a very bad accident scene on the top of that hill!

From that day on, I knew that my life could change at any moment. The awareness of this reality made me desire even more to appreciate every day, and to seek to listen and obey the Lord.

Chapter 6 – Confirmation: God IS in Charge!

A 50 Year Prayer Answered

Before I married Jim, there was a man that I dated that I thought I would marry. He wanted children and we broke up because I told him I did not want to have children. His brother's wife had 3 children, and I was asked to be the God Mother of her first son, Pat, before I realized 'my not wanting to have children' was a deal breaker for that man. After we broke up, he married a lovely woman and had 2 children.

I attempted to visit my God Son, but I was told to stop visiting him, as I had no place now in that 'family.' I would be 50 years before God would arrange for me to meet my God child, Pat. My life continued, and I prayed for all of them.

One of the reasons I never had children was because I was told the earth was 'overpopulated' and people should stop having babies. I thought if that is true, I should adopt and not have children, and so while I was just a teenager, I decided I would never have children.

Time moved on, and both of Pat's parents died, first the mother than the father. One day as I prayed for my God child and the other boys, I told the lord, "You need to send someone to speak to the boys and let them know about Jesus! I would go myself, but I don't think I can just go and knock on their door – I am a complete stranger to them!"

No Coincidences

At that time, I was visiting a nursing home and sharing Jesus with people I met with gift bags and small tokens, as well as fresh fruit and nuts!

The next week as I left visiting that nursing home, I met a woman also leaving. As I talked and shared the love of God with her, she asked, "Are you a minister?" I replied, 'No, I come to visit because I have a friend whose mom is here." She said, "Would you visit my husband next time you come and pray with him?" I replied, "Yes, I can do that!" She told me his name was 'Al', and the next time I stopped to ask the nurse which room he was in. I got the room number and went to visit Al in that room. There was a man in a wheelchair next to the entrance with his back to me and I asked, "Are you Al?" He replied, "He is in the next bed." I said, "Thank you!" and went around the curtain to see a man missing half a leg, and with his arm in a sling. I said, "Your wife Brenda, asked me to stop and see you today, you look like you could use some cheering up!" He replied, "I do! Thank you so much for stopping." We chatted, and before I left, I said, "Would you like me to pray with you before I go?" He replied, "Yes!" I prayed and said, "Shall I come again next week?" He replied, "Please stop anytime! It was great to meet you!"

As I went to leave, I decided to chat with his roommate and leave him a little bible and a small eagle. As I placed my hand on his back and got in front of him, I asked him, "Would you like something to cheer you up today?" He replied, "Sure!" As I handed him the gift pack, I said, "Can you promise me you will read this?" He said, "I'll look at it." I asked, "What's your name?
He replied, "Pat."

I looked at him, he was quite young, and he made me think of my God son Pat. I said, "What's your last name?" He gave me his last name. I was stunned. I looked at his face. I could see his mother and father in his face, and I knew that this was my Pat! I said, "I have something to tell you that is going to seem unbelievable. I knew your mom and Dad." He replied, "Really?!" I then told him the whole story, and told him he was looking at his 'God Mother'. Both of us were speechless. I said, "I will stop again."

The next week when I stopped, he was no longer in that room. Al told me he had been moved into his room the very day I arrived, just a couple of hours before I got there, and then was taken out of the room after I left. I went asking for Pat and they had moved him to the other side of the building. I realized that the odds of our meeting were totally in the hands of the Lord!

I continued to bring him snacks and nuts, and then COVID hit, and I was not allowed to visit. When COVID started to lift, I went again but was told he had died. I contacted the family, and they told me when the memorial service would be held.

It was a very snowy day but my second husband, Fabien agreed to drive me to Fletcher to that service.

We were greeted warmly. Pat had told his brothers and family about me, and they were receptive to the bible book and the mini eagles that I gifted each of them that day.

The Lord had answered my 50-year prayer in such an incredible way!

Pat was in heaven with many other friends of mine!

It took 50 years for the Lord to provide an answer to my prayer!

We are assured that the Lord 'honors those who honor Him."

This miraculous experience is truly evidence of the truth of God's faithfulness to us! God DOES hear and he DOES answer prayers!

Chapter 7 – Visitations from Above

My First After Death Visitation

One of the friends that I met at Faith Baptist Church was Pattie. We were very close and one day she did not feel well. She had cancer and although it looked like they had gotten it, she ended up going home to Jesus. Her last words to me were, "Live your life dawn, don't worry about what people think!" She said, "I am going to come back to you after I die!" I told her, "I don't think you will be allowed to do that but tell Jesus I said Hi for me!' She told me she would, and the evening of the day she died, Pattie did come back to me in a bubble above my bed - her blonde hair blew back away from her face and she said, "It's Beautiful" and then as quickly as the bubble had popped into the room, it receded back and disappeared. And she was not the only one to come to me that way!

My Second After Death Visitation

When I was working with teachers, one of them came to my desk one day and said, "Do you believe like Kay believes?" I had heard Kay telling Barbara about Jesus and she did not like it at all. I replied, "I am afraid I do!" Barbara left that day very angry with both of us. But I started praying for her – and one day Barbara came back into my office and said, "I am here to pray with you." I replied, "I don't think I can pray with you Barbara. Do you believe that Jesus came, and died and rose again?" She replied, "Yes, I do!" I got up from my desk and went to the outside counter area and gave her a hug and said, "Let's pray!" She repeated the same prayer I had said so long ago, and I told her 'These things are! written that you may **_KNOW_** that you have 'eternal life'!"

And, "Whosoever calls upon the name of the Lord shall be saved." We hugged again and she left. I had no idea how sick she was, but she died soon after. And the night of the day she died, she came to me in the same bubble. When I saw her, I said, "Barbara, your dead!" But she reached through the bubble and hugged me and said, "Thank you!" And then the bubble and her presence was gone as quick as it came. I knew that she knew that I had been praying for her and that the Lord allowed her to let me know that I need to keep praying!

After Death Confirmation

I would meet another man who had been in a motorcycle accident and was paralyzed from his waist down. Kevin was very unhappy. He had been brought to a 'fair' and was in his wheelchair when we met. I realized that he lived a short distance away from the home that I had been able to purchase that would become a home for both myself and my father. I would stop to visit him in his home on my way to my home from work to encourage him to have faith. Three years would pass, and one day I called him and asked him if he had read any of the Bible that I had left him. He had not. I said, "Kevin, would you be willing to pray with me on the phone?" He replied, "Yes." Kevin asked the Lord to forgive him and to come into his heart. But the very next day, I would learn that Kevin had taken his life. I was on assignment caring for an older woman and got up in the middle of the night to use the bathroom. As I sat and looked out the window, I told Kevin, "It is so unfortunate that you did that!" Then, suddenly I heard Kevin's voice! he said, "You have no idea how VAST it is!" The Lord had honored his prayer and he was in heaven!

Chapter 8 – The Outing

Buried Memories

After my friend Pattie Pratt had died, I was very sad and upset and went for 'grief counseling'. When I arrived, I was called to a room that had one window and one door and the man that was talking with me had an unusually big nose. I felt very 'unsafe' and did not hear anything he said to me. I wanted to be out of that room. Finally, the session was over and I went home. Once home, I sat on our couch and wondered, "Why were you so upset? You were perfectly safe!"

I told the Lord, "I need to know what is going on here." I determined to just sit on our couch until I knew why I was so scared. Time passed and nothing happened. I decided this was crazy and got up to go to the kitchen but stopped and turned around. I made myself sit back down on that couch. There was a catalog on the coffee table, and I picked that up, but made myself put it down. I sat with nothing to do for a very long time. Then suddenly without warning I saw a vision of 'myself' at 11 years old trapped in a 'bedroom that had one window and one door with a man that was chasing me around the room.' I would remember more of the event but realized that I had been molested when I was 11 by one of our neighbors. I was babysitting their children, and I had arrived to babysit, and there was only the man in the house. He had lured me to go upstairs by telling me," I want to show you something!" Thinking the kids were upstairs, I climbed the steps and went into the top bedroom. When I realized the kids were NOT there, he told me to go and look out the window which I did.

When I turned around, I watched as he closed the door.
I was trapped.

Once I remembered being molested by that neighbor, everything started to make more sense in my life. I had buried the pain. He told me he would kill me if I ever told anyone.

I had been so terrified, and I had buried the memory and chose to never think of it again! But this buried pain did not 'go away' – it now would have to be dealt with. This incident would cause me to understand. This was the reason for my difficulty connecting with my then husband Jim.

The remembrance of my molestation would become a 'wall' to my marriage to Jim, and I would eventually announce to him, "I love you, but I have to leave." He agreed thinking I would be gone for a while and come back. I went and lived with my sister back on our home farm. I was unable to trust men and would 'run' when I felt like I was not able to be in control. We did not use any lawyers, and got a divorce, but we are still friends to this day.

Jim would end up caring for his parents in their home, I would end up caring for my dad in my home, I would end up dating many men, but realizing that I needed divine healing if I was to ever be married again.

Chapter 9 – Courage in Action

A Life Saved

When I married Jim, he was an electrical technician but soon after our marriage he decided to follow in his father's footsteps and become a Police Officer. As a Police Officer he faced many difficult situations, but one of them would allow him to save a boy's life!

On that particular day, I had decided to go home for lunch and after I had finished my meal inside, as I got into my car to leave, suddenly, Jim drove in to the driveway in his police cruiser.

We had never met like this before! I rolled down my window and said, "Well, there we agree on one thing! Lunch at home!" We both laughed. "How's your day going?" he asked. I replied, "Well, I get to see you! So, I would say it is going great!" He said," See you later tonight!" I rolled up my window and drove out of the driveway.

As I looked in my rear- view window, I saw him get out of his police cruiser. As soon as I had left our driveway, Jim heard a huge explosion across the street. He ran into our neighbor's back yard to see 3 boys standing around a fire, and one of them was 'on fire'!

The boy on fire had taken a paint spray can and had sprayed it onto the fire and the fire had travelled back through the air to the can in his hand which exploded into his body. Jim called 911 as he ran to him and then pushed him to the ground and rolled him over and over to get the flames out, burning his own hands. He quickly picked the boy up and carried him into the house and put him in the bathtub and turned on the faucet, running cold water on him.

The ambulance arrived and transported the boy to the emergency room at the hospital. The boy was burned on 80% of his body and doctors were unsure he could recover from the skin grafts needed. Prayers were made for him and miraculously the boy did survive.

Many years later, I would be at the hairdressers and would give a Christian poem to the woman beside me who exclaimed, "I remember you! Your husband saved that boy's life –he is a hero! Did you know that boy is now an officer as well, because of that event?" I did not know that but said, "Yes, my husband Jim was truly a remarkable man!"

Jim was never recognized for what he did, but he will be when we get to heaven. I also knew something else. Te 'time' that we spent just chatting in the driveway' had given him enough time to still be outside and not inside the house when the explosion occurred – which gave him enough time to take the required action to put the fire out and get him into cold water in that bathtub!

The Coming DIVINE Accounting
Chapter 10 – Unexpected Blessings

After my divorce, I longed to have a home again. My father, suggest I build a house for him and me on the land that he owned where his trailer was located. But I would not be able to build on his land because of issues with deeding that land back to him with one of my sisters.

My Dad was now having trouble doing stairs and told me to come and look at the house in Highgate which was perfect for him and me.

The home had an entrance that did not have any entrance stairs on the lower level, and it had an upper level where I could live and be able to provide help for him when he needed it. When the owners of the Highgate property called and told me they were interested in selling, I was working to have enough money to purchase it. I had purchased a condo and was able to sell it and come up with more money needed to buy the house, but when they decided to sell all of the land, I ended up short by $25,000. It would be a call from my Fidelity representative that would tell me I could borrow that exact amount, and the check arrived the day before the closing – enabling me to complete the purchase.

Dawn Densmore-Parent

Chapter 11 – The Divine Meeting

God Heals Broken Hearts

God wants us to heal, and I kept praying for God to help me to be able to forgive the man who molested me. This was very hard to do but I longed to be 'free' from fear and hate. One day, while I was at work, I was asked me to go to the Burlington Post office to mail a package. When I arrived, I noticed in the line in front of me was the man who molested me. I felt my body temperature get very 'hot' but realized he was ahead of me by 3 people and would be out of the P.O. before I was through mailing the package at the counter. I watched as he completed his transaction and went to leave and I walked up to the counter to be served. When I was through and turned to leave, I looked and there he was standing at the entrance holding the door 'for me'.

When I got to the door, he said, "A gentleman always opens the door for a lady!" I replied, "I am a lady but you are anything but a gentle man! Do you know who I am?" He replied, "No!" I said, "I am Dawn Palmer, the little girl you molested when I was just a child!" He was shocked, "I have been to counseling for that!" Now a line was forming behind us. and we were both blocking the entrance and the exit as we shouted at each other! Some clapped and said, "You go!" I replied, "Counseling doesn't change anything for me, you ruined my life!" On that, I exited the 2nd door and went to my car and sat and cried.

I had seen and talked to my molester. It was totally unexpected and uncanny to have been asked to go to that P.O. just when he was there in line! Only God could orchestrate that! I started praying for him and asked the Lord to help me to forgive him.

A Repeat Meeting

Years went by. I was working weekends to earn more money to be able to finish the downstairs of the Highgate home for my dad and was doing in-house care for older people who needed help. I was assigned to take an older couple out to eat on Christmas Eve. They asked to go to Trader Dukes. When we arrived, the restaurant had a buffet meal for patrons. I asked where they wanted to be seated. They asked to sit in the booths across from the bar stools. So, I got them settled into the booth they had picked. As I looked at the bar stool adjacent to that table, on that bar tool sat my molester. There was a mirror in front of the bar, so I could see his face. He had on blue jeans and a white tee shirt with sleeves rolled up and he had dyed his hair black. He was very old, and his arm muscles were no longer firm; he looked pretty horrible. When I sat down, my face became 'white'. The couple asked if I was okay. I replied, 'The man who molested me is seated right there on that bar stool across from us!" They were shocked! "What are you going to do?" I replied, "Nothing!" But as we ordered I could see his face in that mirror. He was looking at something in the corner of the restaurant. I looked to see what he was looking at, but it did not take long to figure that out, it was a young girl about 11 who was in a short sleeve dress.

The Coming DIVINE Accounting

When she stood to go to the buffet and as she walked, his eyes followed her and his head turned to keep his eyes on her.

I could see he was truly 'imprisoned by the 'lust of his flesh' and not free at all! And I realized that I was 'free" even to be able to forgive him! As we finished our meal, he got up to leave and turned and said, "Have a good day!" As he walked away, I knew I had to follow him and tell him that I had forgiven him.

A Mad Dash

I had to run to catch up to him before he exited. I called his name, "Donald, wait!" He stood and turned around and snarled, as he recognized me. He said, "You! What do YOU want?"

I replied, "I want to tell you I have forgiven you!" He replied, "Is that it?" I said, "I want to give you this tract." He said, "What do I do with this?" I said, "I suggest that you read it and say the prayer on the back of it!" He said, "Is that it!" I said, "Yes!" and I walked back to the booth.

The couple wanted to know what I said to him, and I told them, I said, "I told him that I have forgiven him!"

They were amazed, and so was I!

The Lord had gifted me that year for Christmas – freedom from hatred and from bondage to that hatred, that created a barrier in my heart that I had towards all men.

Chapter 12 – God's Divine Answers

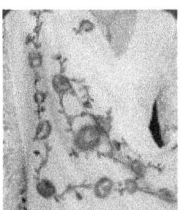

The Importance of Praying

With so many answered prayers, I was motivated to get up every morning to make sure I was praying for people that I loved and for people I had met. To accomplish this task, I began taking more time, and I began to rotate my prayer list to pray through the prayer books that I had made of people that I was meeting.

But one day as I began to go down through that listing, I stopped. I looked up to heaven and told Jesus, "I think I am overdoing this prayer thing! Some of these people I have not met in years, and I don't even know if they are alive anymore -look at H. G. I met her in an elevator at the hospital, and she had just lost her husband, and that was a very long time ago – I bet she is not even alive anymore!" On that I closed my prayer book as I thought to myself, "You make such a BIG deal about everything, you really do take things too far!" That very day I would end up in the Ben Franklin Store and behind a woman with a beautiful Shaul that was embroidered. It was so stunning I said, "That Shaul you are wearing is very beautiful!" As I listened to her reply, I realized I recognized the very voice of H.G. When she finished talking, I said, "I believe I know you, you are H.G. and we met in an elevator at the hospital and your husband had just died."

She turned quickly and looked at me, "Yes, I remember you! That was a very long time ago! How did you know it was me!" I told her I recognized her voice but I did not tell her about my conversation with God. We parted and I knew the Lord had arranged for us to meet to confirm to me that He did want me to pray for people that he placed in my life.

The Prayer for a new Black Skirt

It seems there is nothing that the Lord cannot do! One time when I realized I needed a new black skirt, I went through a Penney's catalog and looked at the price of one and decided I could live with the one I had.

I held up the catalog to heaven and said, "Lord if you want me to have a black skirt, you will have to give one to me. I am not buying one!" I tossed out the catalog and laughed as I thought about my saying that to the Lord.

But that very Sunday after church my friend Lynne, asked me to wait before I left. She said, "Wait, I have something for you!" She then handed me a bag with not 1 but 2 black skirts! She had no idea I had said that prayer and was just as shocked as I was when I told her about it.

God's Unconditional Love - The HIPPO

One of the things that brought me great comfort was a tangible reminder that I was loved. I did not think I was 'good enough' to be loved. One day I said, "I do not understand, Lord, how You, who are Lord, can love 'me!'"

I felt the Lord ask me, "What is the ugliest animal in the world?"

I replied, "A hippopotamus!" The Lord responded, "Well, hippos are beautiful to me!" From that point on, I understood that if God loved something that I thought was the ugliest thing in the world, then He must be able to love me just like that too! From that point forward, when people found out that I liked hippos, they would give one of them to me!

One of my favorite stuffed hippos, I would bring with me to sleep with me when I was doing overnight assignments for older people in their homes. That stuffed hippo gave me comfort at night when I was in a home, I was unfamiliar with, when I did home care on nights and weekends.

The Smallest Hippo in the World

It was during a trip that I needed change for a 'parking meter' that I noticed a display of tiny rubber animals, that included a tiny hippopotamus at the checkout register.. I had put a large hippo on the dashboard of my car, so I got 3 baby hippos to go under that hippo.

The Synchronistic 'Gift' of a Baby Hippo

Soon after, while talking with a passenger during a flight back to Burlington, VT, I was offered a ride to the UVM parking lot by a professor from McGill University. When his wife and daughter arrived to pick him up, as I got into their back seat, I found what I thought was 'a pink stuffed bunny'. Their daughter spelled her name for me, as I picked up the stuffed toy and exclaimed, "What a cute bunny!" I was corrected, "That is not a bunny, it is a hippopotamus! Our daughter just got that yesterday as a gift!" His daughter then showed me her small rubber rabbit. I said, "Well I have a very small hippopotamus in my car that would be a perfect playmate for your bunny!" When their headlights hit my vehicle, it was obvious a large hippopotamus was on the dashboard. I quickly got one of the baby hippos and handed it to the father through his window. I said, "This is pretty small! I hope I am not creating a problem here!"

A few months later I received an email from that McGill University professor asking if I was the person who gave the hippo to his daughter. He wanted me to know how very special that hippo had become to her!

Chapter 13 – The Divine Assignment

"What Do You Believe?"

One individual I was assigned to care for on weekends had cancer. On the very first day I met W., he asked, "What do you believe?" "I responded, "Thank you for asking, but I am not allowed to talk to you about religion." He replied, "You are working for me, and I asked a question and I want an answer!" He sat up and moved his head closer to me – now we were almost face-to-face as I sat on the edge of his couch and he sat on the edge of his chair. I replied, "Well, I believe in the man who was raised from the dead and who walked through walls, and his name would be Jesus!"

W. leaned closer and said, 'Do you know what people in my field call people like you?" I leaned closer to him and said, "No, what DO people in your field call People like ME?" He raised his voice and shouted, "Delusional!"

I leaned forward and pointed to my head and said, "That is because faith is not from your **HEAD** but from your **HEART**!" I said this as I pointed to my own heart. He had no answer but in the weeks, and months that followed he would try to engage me in arguing with him, but I refused. Instead, I prayed for him.

He had a Chaplin that would visit him who would share the Bible with him, and they would argue back and forth. I knew God would have to do something BIG to melt this man's iceberg of unbelief.

A Miracle

One day on my shift he asked me to take him to the hospital. He had lost sight in one of his eyes. I prayed, "Lord, he has so much to deal with right now, please heal him! Please don't add this to his plate!" Before we could even get into the car, he told me suddenly he could see again out of that eye. We went anyway to have his eye checked and they found nothing. I thanked the Lord for this miracle.

Later I would also take him to a regular visit to his doctor, and on that visit, he had an accident in his pants. We were told there was a bathroom he could use in the doctor's office. This bathroom was very small. We both just barely fit in there together, but he needed me with him in that bathroom to be able to help him.

I worked to get his soiled underwear off and tied off and placed into the trash bin, and that also got tied closed. Things were going well, but now he had no underwear on. I told him to wait before he pulled his pants up. He was concerned about another accident. I went and asked the nurse for the blue liner that was on the counter. She unloaded what was on top and handed it to me. When I came back with that liner, he asked, "What are you going to do with that?' I said, "I can place it between your legs and when you pull your pants up, it will protect your pants!"

As I worked, I said, "You know, everything that happens down here on earth has a lesson in it!" He replied, "And just WHAT would this LESSON be?!" "I replied, "I am very honored to be able to help you W., and this lesson would be about 'humility' and there is nothing about 'that' that you can be proud of; so this is a lesson in what Humility looks like.

I could tell that W. finally understood! It was his own "Helen Keller" moment! Helen Keller was blind but understood the word 'water' when her hand was placed under water when the word 'water' was spoken. W. understood the link between the material and spiritual world for the first time!

W. continued to decline. The last time I saw him; I knew that I would NOT see him again on earth. That morning before I left to go to work, I prayed as I wanted to share my faith with him. Suddenly I realized I could gift him the 'hippo' that I slept with. I took my stuffed hippo and brought it to him as he laid in his hospital bed that was now in his living room.

I said, "W, I have a gift for you!" He took it and held it up and said, "And WHAT is this!" I replied, "It is my sleeping hippo, and I have slept with every night that I have been here. It is my comfort, and I want to give that to you." He smiled and took it. I said, "Would you like to pray with me?" He smiled and said, "Yes!" And right there he repeated a prayer professing his faith in Jesus and asking Jesus to forgive him for his unbelief!

He would pass that very week. When I told my caregiver friend who was with him before he died, about my gift and his prayer with me, she replied, "Is that WHAT that was! You have no idea! W. had to have that every time we moved him, he asked for it to hold it." We both were touched. I attended his memorial service. His minister told everyone, :W. was a professed atheist" As I sat in that pew, I wept. I knew W. was in heaven.

The Remarkable Confirmation

Three years later, I was assigned to care for a woman whose husband had to be placed into a home. As I made her dinner, I noticed a picture of W. in her home. I also saw a photograph of a man that looked very familiar to me.

After dinner I asked her, "Who is that man in the picture I think I know him!" She replied, "That is my husband!" I asked, "Why do you have a picture of W. in your house?" She replied, "He was my husband's best friend!"

Suddenly, I knew I had to tell her that I knew that W. was in fact in heaven. She replied, "I know that! You need to know that W. appeared to my husband after he died and told him, "Thank you!" But you need to go and tell my husband your account though, he will love to hear of it from you."

The next day I went to see the minister in the nursing home. As I told him my account, that minister held up his hand and 'waved' to W. and said, "Buddy, I will see you soon!"

The minister's doctor walked in as he held his hand up and said that. I turned and handed that doctor a Biblical tract and said, "It is great to know where you are going when you die! " The physician replied, "Yes! Thank you!"

The Coming DIVINE Accounting

Chapter 14 – Yielded to Divine Guidance

Two Divine Meetings – 50 Years Apart

I told one of Fabien's great-grandchildren, "You know I met your great grandpa when I was just a teenager. We went to the same school, and he used to flirt with me, and I loved his blue eyes and blonde hair."

The school we went to had a hallway with an opening between two areas. We were told not to go beyond an invisible divide between the 7-8 graders and the High School students' areas. But the boy with the blue eyes and blonde hair wore white pants to school and would come down the stairs and turn and put his foot against the wall and look at me, and I at him. My heart would skip a beat each time we got to see each other after classes before we went home.

We never talked to one another, because of that invisible divide between us. When I got to High School, I had a best friend who told me that she was in love with a man who wrote notes to her. And it turned out that Fabien was that man! Fabien married another Debbie. After that year, I would never see him again but always wondered about the guy with the white pants, and blonde hair and blue eyes that I had a crush on. It would be nearly 50 years later when Fabien and I realized all of this as we talked.

Dawn Densmore-Parent

The night before our 8th wedding anniversary we chatted about our younger years. We both realized it was Fabien that I had a crush on in 8th grade!

Time marches on! When I met Fabien, he had been single 18 years, and I had been single 23 years! I met Fabien again because of a friend who suggested that I check out Christian singles. I told her, "Because you are suggesting it, I will do it!" When I got home that Friday I did a search for 25 miles from my home. I had to post a picture of myself in order to gain access to do a search on their web site. As I did a search for 25 miles from my home, suddenly a man sent a "wink" at me. That man was Fabien who was located just 8 miles away. I 'winked' back, but we both had to join to talk.

Fabien visited me at my home, and we liked one another right away, but he wanted someone to live on his farm with him and I wanted someone to marry and come and live with me and my dad in Highgate. We dated on and off for 5 years. I still had 'control' issues and I prayed about Fabien.

One night I had a dream that he and I were at church and had left and were descending some steep stairs. He was holding my hand, and I looked back to see a little girl behind us who was stuck on the steep stairs. She could not get down the steps. I stopped and let go of Fabien's hand and went back to help that little girl. I said to her, "I am here to help you, you don't need to be afraid!"

As the little girl looked up to me, I could see Fabien come back up the stairs to help her as well. Now both of us together helped her. As I looked back into the face of that little girl, I realized the little girl was me! Then, suddenly, I woke up! it was a dream!

But I KNEW this dream was from God, who was letting me know that Fabien was safe and that I did not need to be afraid of him. God had gifted me a dream to show me that!

 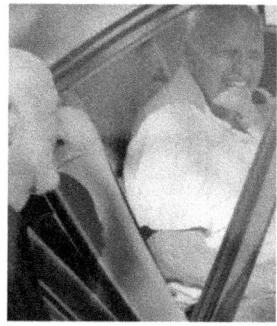

Farm Wedding - September 19, 2015

While on a date In 2015 Fabien asked me, "What would you say if I asked you to marry me?"

I touched his forehead and said, "Are you sick?" But no, he was serious! We married the day before his birthday on Sept. 19, 2015.

My dad made it to our wedding that was on Fabien's farm. After our honeymoon in Lake Placid, New York, Fabien moved in with me to Highgate Center and sold his farm to one of his sons.

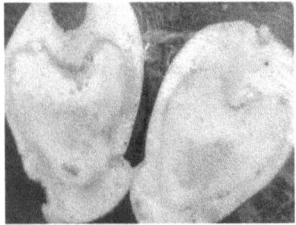

The "Heart" Egg

Fabien brought such joy and peace into my life. One Valentine's Day I told the Lord I wanted to give something to Fabien that was 'special' but that would cost nothing. As I prayed, I thought of making him deviled eggs! When I started to cut them open, one of the eggs had a 'perfect heart' inside the shell.

I stood and looked at it in 'disbelief' and set that egg aside – I would leave it as it was! I placed that egg on his plate and handed the plate to him for supper that night. He said, "**That must have been a very happy chicken to lay such a lovely egg!**" We both laughed!

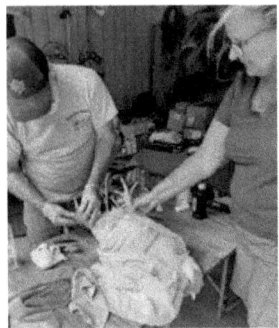

The Rooster Operation.

Our neighbor's chickens and rooster were 'free range' and spent most of their days in our yard, and we loved having them along with the turkeys that she had.

Fabien kept an eye on the farm animals. He was good at 'seeing' things that needed attention. One day Fabien noticed our neighbor's rooster was standing a lot on one foot. Fabien was able to go and pick him up and discovered he had 'bumble foot'.

Our neighbor agreed to help Fabien remove that from his foot. The rooster was named, "Sad Sam". Fabien cut a clear plastic bag, and I held the bag as he placed Sad Sam head down into the bag.

We expected a 'fight' but Sad Sam – did not move.

As he was held, Fabien began the 'operation' to remove the infection as our neighbor held Sad Sam. This procedure would occur again and again until Fabien got to the 'core' and removed it out of his foot. Then it would take several months for Sad Sam's foot to heal.

And Sam had a small hen that would come and stand next to the calf hutch that we had placed him in for his 'hospital' room. Fabien placed that small hen inside with him, so he was not alone. In the end, the operation was a success.

We renamed 'Sad Sam' – 'Happy Sam', and he got to enjoy being alive a lot longer.

Dawn Densmore-Parent

Chapter 15 - Yielded

The Vision

The real 'purpose' of being alive on earth came to me one morning when I was reading the Bible. Jesus had answered a question on what the greatest commandment was, by saying, "Love the Lord Your God with all your heart, with all your soul, with all your strength and with all your might and the second is like the first, love your neighbor as yourself."

As I sat and pondered His answer, I remembered another Bible verse: "Straight is the gate and narrow is the way that leadeth unto life." Suddenly a white light appeared straight down in front of me, which was crossed by another horizontal 'light' and then where those lights met, came a HUGE burst of LIGHT in the Center – it looked just like the CROSS Jesus died on

I understood that 'Loving God' was the vertical line; and 'Loving Others' was the horizontal line - and when done together, these brought us into the very 'power' of God, who is able to do GREAT things in answer to our prayers!

We would experience this very 'power' in action soon after!

My Unexpected Mission

I signed up to go on a mission trip to Wales but two weeks before the trip, I knew that the Lord did not want me to go on that trip. It was very hard for me to do, but I emailed our Pastor and told him I could not go on this mission's trip – and then asked him to gift it to someone who could go in my place.

I would end up meeting the very person who was 'gifted' the trip in the Ladies Room of our church about 2 weeks later. As we talked, she exclaimed, "And I am going to Wales!"

I replied, "How wonderful! I was going to go on that trip, but I had to cancel." She then was very quiet, and said, "I have something to tell you! I am the person who is going in your place!" We both hugged and I said, "I am so glad you are able to go, I will be praying for you!"

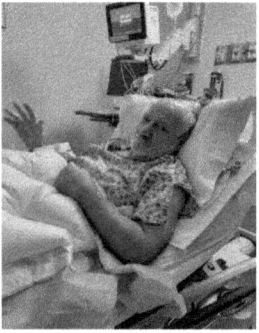

The Unexpected Event

Fabien would experience a 'stroke' on the day of our 8th wedding anniversary. I called our pastor for prayer, and after he prayed for us on the phone, he said, "Aren't you glad you are not here in London! We just landed today. You would have had to fly back!"

I had completely forgotten about the trip! Fabien's stroke caused him to lose feeling on his left side. His left arm, hand and leg and foot no longer responded to his brain – he could not move them.

Many prayers were made, and he was approved for rehabilitation therapy, and was able to regain use of his entire left side. Tests had been done that revealed that Fabien had 'masses' in his bladder, and surgery was scheduled. The tumors were removed, and he remained in the hospital for 2 nights before discharged to come home on Christmas Eve.

We no sooner got to bed than he sat up and told me to take him back to the hospital. Instead of driving him, I dialed 911 and an ambulance arrived to bring Fabian to the hospital. I was told to follow the ambulance, but when it sped up beyond my ability to follow, I prayed out loud, "Lord, please don't take my Fabien!"

When I got to the hospital Emergency Room, I was told "Your husband has had a severe heart attack during transport." It would be 48 hours before Fabien would have triple bypass surgery.

The surgeon informed us that even the operation might not work, as his heart appeared to be severely damaged. Prayers were made by many people, and I began fasting and praying for him.

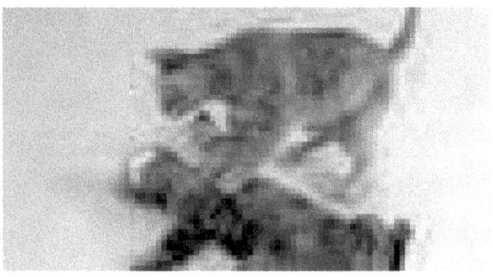

A Visual of Healing

An image of an orange cat giving 'resuscitation to a tiger cat was texted to me by one of my sisters that I received right after I had seen an 'image' of Fabien in the arms of Jesus while praying.

Fabian survived and recovered from the stroke, the heart attack, and surgery for removing the masses from his bladder cancer, and from the chemo treatments. It would be a little over a year later that we would receive the news that Fabien was free of cancer.

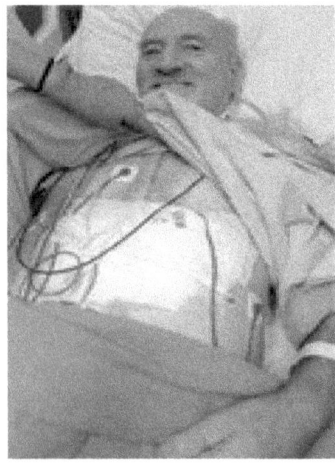

Chapter 16 – The Supernatural

Visions

My life also included not only 'dreams' but also 'visions' that I kept 'secret'. These occurred at times when I was totally discouraged, and the Lord gave them to me to encourage me.

One night I would find myself in front of a throne in heaven and I would be given a 'vision' like a 'movie' of my entire life. I was told, "You will remember being here, but you will not remember seeing these things." Then I was immediately 'back inside my body' and I was in bed in my bedroom. Then, suddenly I heard someone clapping their hands beside my bed. CLAP, CLAP, CLAP! As I heard each loud 'Clap', I also heard a voice from the side of my bed say: "Let's go! Let's go! Let's go!" Then, a force pulled me physically out of the bed and onto the floor!

Once again there were electrical shocks that I felt go through my back as I felt an entity push me and squash me into the floor. I prayed for the Lord to make the entity go away! It seemed like a long time but finally that entity left and I was free! I got up off the floor and got back into my bed. The whole experience was beyond what I could understand.

I told the Lord, "I have no idea what all of this means, but thank you Lord that you are with me!"

After this experience, there would be times when I would be able to 'see' in my mind's eye, the very moment I was experiencing, and I would 'know' what would happen next.

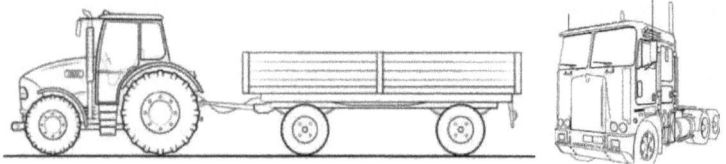

God's Answered Prayer for A Hug

One dream that I experienced seemed real!

In the dream I was driving a big truck and was following a tractor with 2 men on it which had stopped quickly in front of me. As I pushed on the truck brakes, the truck jackknifed and turned backwards and the bed of the truck pulled the entire truck off the road into a huge liquid manure pit that was right by the side of the road. As I sat in the cab of the truck, the liquid manure began to fill the cab. I started shouting, "Get me out of here!" The 2 men that were on the tractor came and opened the truck door and got me out but I was now covered with liquid manure, right up to my neck! I walked with the 2 men to the front of their barn, and they got a hose to hose me off. My clothes were so bad they had to be removed, so there I stood before these 2 men, totally naked. I could see them 'laughing' as they told they would go and get some clothes for me. As they left, I could see a very large tree next to the house, and I went to sit down at the base of that tree. I pulled up my legs with my arms around my legs and up to my chest, and comforted myself, "You are Okay. You will have some clothes soon. Everything is okay!"

As I sat under that tree, I looked up into the blue sky. It was a beautiful day! Then, suddenly I saw a chariot and a rider in the sky with a white horse galloping and pulling the chariot across the sky. The tree I was under was located near a road and cars were travelling north and south on that road. I wondered if the people travelling in those cars could see the chariot and rider, too?

Then that chariot driver started to turn his horse in a circle that was coming my way. I knew that he would be travelling right behind the big tree I was sitting under. I immediately stood up and walked out from away from the base of the tree so I could see that chariot come back out around the top branches of the tree – and it DID!

As I watched the driver suddenly turned again and the horse and the chariot now came right down and landed on the ground right in front of me! The chariot driver immediately got off and came and gave me a BIG hug!

I said, "O take me with you, now!" But suddenly I opened my eyes, and no one was there! I knew that it had been a dream, yet I could still feel the imprint of the arms on my back of that driver that had just hugged me!

I had prayed to the Lord the day before, "Lord, I need a hug, and not a Pansy hug, but a REAL hug from a strong man!"

I had no expectation that my 'prayer' would be answered in such an amazing way, but God had provided me comfort amid a very trying time, in a very miraculous dream.

Dawn Densmore-Parent

Confirmation from the Lord

A week would pass, and I would visit one of my sister's homes. She had a framed picture on her counter and that picture was a perfect match of the sky and land that I had seen in my dream. The only thing that was missing in the picture was the 'chariot 'being pulled by the white horse with the chariot driver and his robe flying in the wind behind him in the sky!' She, without my asking for it, offered me that picture! I knew the Lord was using that painted picture to assure me that the 'dream' had been from him as well as the 'hug'!

Confirmation of Prayers Answered

One morning as I lay in bed praying about the day, I suddenly heard a bell ringing and then in my mind's eye, a beautiful silver box with diamonds all around the edge of it appeared to me. The box suddenly had a slit appear down the front of it in the center of the front of the heart and these suddenly opened up like a double door.

I then saw images of people's faces in black and white – faces of people that I did not recognize coming and smiling one right after another - again and again. And then the whole box just disappeared. I opened my eyes and thanked the Lord for encouraging me to continue to share my faith with the people I meet, as many of them I will meet in heaven someday – the Sower and the reaper will rejoice together on that day!

A Divine Sign

My passion is to share Jesus with others, and I have been called, "The God Squad." The lack of enthusiasm for Jesus by others caused me to boldly say, "Lord, let me know if YOU are pleased with me, in a way that is large enough so that I cannot miss it!" It would be the very next day that my youngest sister would visit from Georgia. I would go to see her at my other sister's home. When I arrived, there was a cardboard box set next to her garage. As I went to pick it up to put it to recycle, my youngest sister came around that garage. She said, "O that is for you!" As I opened the box, I could see it was a sign and it said, "**Thank you Jesus**". Tears welled up in my eyes. She said, "We all know you love Jesus, and we thought of you thanking him all the time, so we got you this sign!" I replied, "I actually see this sign very differently, I see this as Jesus saying, "Thank you" signed "Jesus." This truly was something I could not miss! We still have this sign! It has had to be repaired and reinforced, but I love it!

Dawn Densmore-Parent

Chapter 17 – Be Prepared

The Rapture

As I continued to read and study the Bible, I told Jesus, "One thing that I struggle with is the account of Your return in the air known as the Rapture!" I wondered over and over just how THAT would happen! Soon thereafter, I was assigned to care for a man in his home on an overnight assignment. I would again sleep on the floor to make sure I was close enough to be able to assist him if he needed my help at night. My routine was to get up early each day to read my bible, and get ready myself, so that I would be ready to care for him. One morning after I had gotten up, I could hear noises outside the window in the air.

It sounded like 'musical trumpets' blaring. I wanted to go to look out the window to see if I could see what was going on, but before I could do that, suddenly I felt my body lifted up into the air and pulled right up through the roof into the sky. I had put my coat on in the house and now I could see the sky all around me and it was filled with people who had also been pulled up! I shouted, "It's the Rapture!"

Then suddenly – I felt my chest and I realized I was actually lying on the floor. But there was energy within me that was so strong that I jumped up off that floor and started jumping up and down in my pajamas in the living room.

!

What had happened? It had been so 'real' but I apparently 'dreamed' it! The reality of a rapture where believers will be taken up into the sky recorded in the Bible was forever answered for me! There will be a catching away of people in the future that will take everyone by surprise

The Importance of Living Each Day Well

Fabien and I have been truly blessed by the people who have come into our lives. Our friends, Caroline Deloreto and Adam Taft totally reflected God's love, and we enjoyed their company. Caroline was diagnosed with cancer, and one of the last images I have of her is of having her feet sitting on a coffee table that Fabien had saved from being burned – they had asked to have it for a coffee room table and Fabien had repaired its lift top. This coffee table was perfect for her to place her feet on to get some rest from 'coughing' in that position. Her legacy of faith in the midst of her trials encourages those who knew her, to live each day the best that you can, as none of us is assured of any tomorrow. I did hear her call my name, 'Dawn' one morning after she had passed! I look forward to seeing her again when I get there! Adam continues to miss her presence but continues to get up and do his best every day! Each of us is a role model of how to meet adversity in this life. This life is ONLY the beginning of 'eternal' life in heaven with the Lord.

The Communion Cups

One of the most remarkable events in my life came from my friend who is blind. I met her when I worked at UVM, she worked in an adjacent building. She went in for an operation and ended up totally blind. When I learned of this, I volunteered to help her get groceries once a week. We did that 'grocery run' without fail, every week for 18 years until COVID arrived. I missed only 1 time and that was due to a co-worker interrupting my work schedule, The Lord arranged for my blind friend to receive an apology from that person.

At the end of our getting groceries one week, a fire alarm went off in her building which caused us to have to exit her condo complex and go and stand outside on the sidewalk. While we were waiting for the building to be checked out, that very co-worker came walking down the sidewalk, and came over to talk with us. I explained to her that this was the very individual that caused me to not show up when I said I would. He was shocked, and said to my friend, "I had no idea I had caused that issue; I am truly sorry that happened!"

Then one day after a grocery trip, she handed me a bag that had things in it to take to Good Will. When I got home, I went through the bag to clean things before I dropped them off and found 2 chalices.

As I worked to clean them, I realized just one cleaning would not do the trick, so I placed both of them on the counter next to my sink and went to get our mail at the Post Office.

When I re-entered my home, one of the chalices looked like a light was on inside of the 'cup'! I took my camera and took a picture of it and when I looked back – suddenly the light was gone – that one chalice had captured the light of the sun coming through my kitchen window!

This very strange event made me aware that being filled with God's Holy Spirit requires us to be 'clean' and 'available' for God to use us – and that is a CHOICE! There is a little song that says it all: "*Be careful little eyes what you see, be careful little ears what you hear, be careful little hands what you do, be careful little feet where you go -for your Father up above is looking down in love so be careful what you allow to come into your heart and life!* " KEEP your heart and listen and obey the Lord!

When I asked my blind friend if I could keep the chalices, she asked, "What do you want them for?" I replied, "I want them for communion cups in my home!" She was silent for a moment and then replied, "That, was in fact what they were before they were gifted to me at my wedding by the minister that married me!" I said, "Well, it appears they have come 'full circle' as they will again be kept for that use only!"

Remarkable Faith

One woman I was assigned to help in her home, had been through a lot! She had gone in for knee replacement surgery, and there had been a staph infection, that caused both of her legs to have to be removed above the knees. The staff infection continued upward, and her legs were totally removed.

After these operations, she lost her best friend, and another relative also died. I wept with her as she told me these things.
Her life was like "Job" who lost everything at once.

I would stop to see her and send her cards, and one day the Lord told me to go and tell her that "her time was short". I went that very day.

Her caregiver told me not to waste my time, she was nonresponsive! But I knew the Lord would allow me to speak to her, so I went to talk to her anyway. When I called her name, she opened her eyes. I sat in her wheelchair next to her bed, and I told her, "The Lord has sent me to ask you if you still had your faith?" I added, "He has told me to tell you He is coming to take you home!".

She said, "I have NOT lost my faith When is He coming for me? " I replied, "Soon! I have been sent to pray with you."

Then I asked, "Do you believe that Jesus came, died, and is alive forever more?" She replied, "Yes!" She then repeated a prayer with me.

"Jesus I believe you came, and died and are alive, and I ask you to forgive me for the wrong things I have done and come and take me to haven to live with you!"

I said, "I will not see you again down here, but I will see you in heaven!"

I learned that she had been transported that night in an ambulance and had passed on her way to the hospital.

I attended her memorial service. She was a very private person, and her coworkers had no idea what had happened to her. She retired early from her position and that was all they knew.

One person I recognized. I asked, "How do I know you?" She replied, "You stopped at the Fire Department and left me a small hippo, and bible book. Your friend passed on the ambulance I was while we were taking her to the hospital!"

Her testimony is of a person who endured such hardships and yet did not lose faith! Truly, this is truly remarkable faith!

Chapter 18 – The Coming DIVINE Accounting

The Treasure

Jesus talked about a treasure hidden in a field where when it was found, the man sold everything that he had and bought that field. The secret treasure is that we can CHOSE to be like the light in that 'cup' and let God live inside our very heart and guide our very thoughts. When we delight ourselves in the Lord, He GIVES us the desires of our heart! When we acknowledge Him in all that we do, He gives us the strength to do the difficult things that need to be done each day!

Our Divine Partner

When we TRUST him with all our heart and do not LEAN unto our own UNDERSTANDING. He is able to direct our very thoughts. We can have the Lord as our very own skating partner. He skates along beside us and he lifts us UP and spins us around. He works through us to speak to those we meet, and He gives us His words to say that tell of His 'good news' of eternal life in a perfect place. We may find ourselves falling on our 'butts' as He works to get us to be able to learn new things, but the end result is the joy received when we choose to live 'moment by moment' in the very presence of God! His presence is worth every effort and sacrifice!

How to Live in This Current World

We are warned to not set our hearts upon the things of this world for the lust of the flesh, the pride of life and the love of this present world -these are the distractions that 'steal' from us an ability to listen and hear the direction from God's Holy Spirit.

This present world is scaffolding for our eternal soul that lives forever.

So, choose God! Choose to follow and walk in the steps of Jesus Christ! He is indeed the way, the truth and the life – and no man comes to the Father but by Him.

So, choose to love others and no matter what you do –choose to do it with all your heart as unto the Lord and not unto men. Go 'that extra mile' whenever you can!

The Two Accountings

The reason I am sharing these experiences that I have kept 'secret' with you **NOW**, is because of my dream of being in heaven and having my life appear before me. In that space, when I was in line to give an account of my life, as I remembered all these things, I knew I would be told, "*Why did you not share these with me when you were on earth because if you had told me about these things, I would have chosen differently!*" I have been afraid of what people would 'think' of me! But I remember my friend telling me "*Don't worry about what people will think dawn!*" Therefore, I am willing to share all these things, as I know everyone is going to know about them on 'that day' during my own accounting in heaven before the Lord.

Today

Right now, we still can each choose. What will you choose?

I am praying by my sharing my life experiences with you that you will be encouraged to turn to Jesus with all of your heart and tell him you are sorry for not including him in your decisions and ask Him to save you and come into your heart!

The **Lord Jesus will return in the air and that is known as the 'Rapture'.** Those that have died in the Lord will be raised first, then we which are alive and remain will be changed in a moment, in the twinkle of an eye, from corruptible to incorruptible, to meet them in the air, and there shall we ever be with the Lord.

I believe we are now closer than ever to the 'rapture'" It is 'believers' - not the 'bad' people – that Jesus will come to take with him to heaven in the air! Jesus's return in the 'air' will occur suddenly and unexpectedly for all believers. Two shall be grinding at the wheel (daytime), two shall be sleeping in bed (nighttime). There will be the trump of God, and the voice of the arch angel, and then the literal disappearance of all Christ believers.

The End Time Bible Prophecy –Daniel & Revelation

Confusion will follow on earth with explanations that we were taken because we were not ready for the 'great reset' of 'unity' on the earth. A man with incredible charm will come with spiritual powers and will claim to be God. His solutions will seem perfect and wonderful and able to solve all of the earth's problems.

He will create a one world government, a one world currency and a one world religion for all people – but all of these will create 'bondage' not 'freedom.' This new world system requires compliance to a 'man' who will proclaim himself to be the awaited 'Messiah". Rather than 'obedience' out of love for God, this system will be reliant upon the use of Artificial Intelligence, (A.I.) and A.I. does not have a 'heart'.

The new 'one world religion' will teach that everyone is a child of God and 'everyone can be like God".This 'religion' negates the need for the Bible and the record that God came to earth in the form of a man, announced by angels and named, "Jesus" who is alive forever more, and who has paid the debt for all sins on the cross, who was resurrected on the third day and who appeared for 40 days before being taken up into heaven, who will return again after the rapture, at the end of the 7-year tribulation period to set up His Kingdom on earth.

The new 'one world religion' will be based upon the 'good works of men' and not on the 'Grace of God', who sent HIs son Jesus to make a way of escape for WHOSOEVER calls upon His name.

Technology will be able to link each human being to directly connect to a computer with a computer chip in the right hand or in the forehead. People will need to have that in order to buy or sell anything. There will be a false prophet who will confirm that all of this is indeed 'true'. There will be 'aliens' from space craft who will appear on earth to affirm 'humans are indeed 'deity'. The world will accept all of it as the final solution to save the earth.

.

Few will be able to resist the mandatory system worldwide.

Most will gladly report anyone who talks of Jesus being the Messiah. The Jewish nation will rebuild their temple, and 2 witnesses will appear, There will be 144,000 Jewish men that will be from the 12 tribes, 12,000 from each tribe, who will testify to the truth of the Bible..

NOW is the time to receive the Lord! Don't Wait! For Jesus will come as a 'thief in the night' – unexpectedly. The 'times' told to Daniel by the angel, and the visions given to John in the book of Revelation are for 7 years of trouble for the entire world.

Mordecai asked Esther, "Yet who knows whether you have come to the kingdom for *such* a time as this?" At the time, the Jewish nation was threatened by wicked Hamen with extinction. Esther asked her nation to fast and pray for 3 days and 3 nights and then she risked her life and go before the King to plead for her people. Today believers in Jesus Christ find themselves in the exact position of Esther! As for me, I have made my choice!

But the question is, "What will you do?" Are we willing to tell others and those we love about the good news of Jesus Christ? To do as Esther did: to fast, to pray, and to seek others to fast and pray with us and then to be obedient to the leading of God's Holy Spirit moment by moment?! May the Lord Jesus empower us to do so! May the answer be to Jesus's question before he left this earth: "But when I return, will I find faith on earth?" be a resounding "YES! Even so, come Lord Jesus!"

When this corruptible shall put on incorruption and this mortal shall have put on immortality then shall be brought to pass the saying that is written DEATH is swallowed up in victory (1 Corinthians 15:54).

Therefore (because of this) my beloved brethren be ye steadfast, unmovable, always abounding in the work of the Lord for as much as ye know that your labor is NOT in vain in the Lord. (1 Corinthians 5:58). This is the victory that overcomes the world, even our faith.

The 2nd Accounting

The Lord Jesus Christ will return to the earth after the 7-year tribulation period, and there will be a 2nd accounting before the Great White Throne Seat of Christ. There, every person who rejected the message of Jesus Christ, will have their own divine accounting of whatsoever things they have done, whether they were good or bad. The book of life will be opened, and whosoever's name was not written in the Lamb's book of life, will NOT be able to enter due to their own imperfection that has not been covered by the blood of the crucified and resurrected King of King and Lord of Lords. We are told, "Every knee shall bow, and every tongue confess that Jesus Christ is Lord to the glory of God the Father." We are told there will be weeping and gnashing of teeth, as the verdict will be determined by each person's own decision regarding 'eternal life' in a perfect place. At this 2nd accounting the Bible will make perfect sense.

"So then every one of us shall give account of himself to God to God" (Romans 14;12

Chapter 19 – The "Dash"

Each of us has a date of our birth on this earth, and aside from the rapture, each of us will have a date of our death. The question is what are we doing with the 'dash' between these two dates?

One of the most extraordinarily rare events from the Lord in my life came from a 'gift' given to me by my oldest friend Sue!

As I prayed about how to end, "The Trueman Bryer Memory Book", Sue gifted to me a very old book. I had visited her to drop off her birthday present. When I left, she handed me a bag that contained an 1870 book entitled, "Night Scenes in the Bible" by Rev. Daniel March. Knowing my last scheduled time to care for Trueman in his home would be the very next day, I packed the book in my suitcase and looked forward to taking time to read it. I wanted to highlight how this remarkable man was living his 'dash' well!

The Interview

During my first day back with Trueman, I was provided with a book from the family entitled, "Dad Share your Life with Me". My first question to Trueman from that book was, "Please tell me about your family names." Trueman replied, "My Dad's name was 'Charles Truman Bryer'. My dad did not like the name 'Truman', so he was "Charles" and became Charles Truman. When I was born, he wanted to pass the Truman name onto me, but he did not want to spell it 'T R U M A N. He wanted my name to be different, so he spelled my name "True man" or "Trueman" with an 'e' in it. So, my name is "Trueman Earl Bryer". I have no idea what the Earl stands for!"

The 1870 Book Reading

The next morning when I began my Bible reading, I decided to just randomly open the 1870 book, "Night Scenes in the Bible". I opened to Chapter XVI 'A night storm on the sea" (to this excerpt):

"The ship was now in the midst of the sea, tossed with waves; for the wind was contrary. And in the fourth watch of the night Jesus went unto them, walking on the sea" (Matthew XIV 24:25). As I read this chapter, I was totally shocked! 'Trueman's" name was in this chapter. Excerpts from Page 354-365: *When the disciples saw Jesus' walking upon the waves, they thought they saw a spirit, an unreal and ghostly shadow, appearing to terrify rather than to comfort and deliver them. And yet he was the most true and real man that ever walked the earth. . . He is more real, true and satisfying to the earnest, thinking, aspiring mind than wealth or learning or pleasure or power. His grand purpose in all his instructions is to make us **true men** – not angels, not beings destitute of any of the passions, appetites, affections that are essential to our humanity: he would make us **true men**. He stands before us in his human nature, complete, perfect, wanting nothing. And he would make us like himself, true in every purpose, feeling and thought – true in our whole heart and soul and being. This it is to be a **'true man'**. It is to have our whole human nature purified, ennobled, consecrated by the truth. Christian faith, Christian duty, Christian character are at mortal and everlasting enmity with all pretenses, falsehood, and unreality. The man who has the most of the life of Christ in his soul is the most true, genuine and complete man on the face of the earth. To be a Christian it is only necessary to be **a 'true man'** – to love, believe and obey the truth." No man can think of a more desirable close of life for himself than that he may be found faithful to his convictions, true to his own deepest sense of obligation."*

Full Circle Answered Prayer

Equally shocking is the fact that "Sue" who gifted me the 1870's book, is the same "Sue" who asked for blackberries and received blackberries, after she had told the Lord, *"**I do not have time to pick blackberries and if you want me to have them, you will have to give them to me!**"*

The very next day, I was compelled to go and pick 'blackberries' and then compelled to call Sue to ask her if she would be interested in having some blackberries. We were awed at the power of the Lord to answer prayers. Now, as I prayed for a way to wrap up "Trueman Bryer's Memory Book"(to enable readers to understand that the Lord was honoring him), this same person, "Sue" felt compelled to gift me the 1870's book,"Night Scenes in the Bible" that actually contains the message of being a **'true man'** - a **Trueman**! My gift to her back then, had NOW returned full circle:

Sue had prayed for 'blackberries' and I had gifted her the 'blackberries.

I had prayed for the 'book' and Sue had gifted me 'a book' that condenses the entire life of a man of faith named: Trueman: Truly a 'True man".

His 'life' is a legacy of FAITH and LOVE!

Life's ultimate purpose is LOVE. We need GOD's love, present, living within us to be able to OVERCOME this world's jungle of hatred, ingratitude, discouragement, disasters, and dismays. For it is only from God's presence within us that we can:

LOVE where there is 'hate',

FORGIVE when we are offended',

ENCOURAGE those who are 'discouraged',

We are to become a 'vessel' of the LOVE of God to others.

The letters "L – O- V - E" spell out the meaning of life:

God is **LOVE.** (1 John 4:8)

"Beloved, let us love one another for love is of God, and everyone that loveth is of God and is known of God." (1 John 4:7)

"If any man serves me**, him** will my father honor.: Jesus (John 12:26)

"These things have I written unto you that believe on the name of the Son of God; that ye may **know** that ye have eternal life, and **that ye may believe** on the name of the Son of God." (1 John 5:13).

"For God so loved the world that he gave his only begotten son, that whosoever believeth on him should not perish but have everlasting life.

For God sent not his Son into the world to condemn the world, but that the world through him might be saved" (John 3:15-16).

"The word of faith which we preach; that if thou shalt confess with thy mouth the Lord Jesus, and shalt believe in thine heart that God has raised him from the dead, thou shalt be saved.

For with the heart man believeth unto righteousness and with the mouth confession is made unto salvation" (Romans 10:9-10).

For **whosoever** shall call upon the name of the Lord shall be saved" (Romans 10:13).

Dawn Densmore-Parent

Chapter 20 - The Biblical Record

Choose to Read the Bible

"The Coming Divine Accounting" will validate the entire Biblical record. This record is contained in all 66 books of the Bible:39 in the Old and 27 in the New Testament. It is the Words of God. written in the Bible, that will be used during each of our accountings.

"Faith is the substance of things hoped for; the evidence of things not seen." (Hebrews 11:1)

The message of the Bible is one of God's Love for every person! May the Lord give to you a desire to read the Bible for yourself! "For the Truth shall set you FREE!"

The eternal message to us is:
God is Love, God is Truth, God is Spirit. We were created to love God and to love one another. None of us can do this perfectly all the time, so from the beginning of time, a plan was devised to provide for us a way to connect with God and others.

Abraham believed God and it was counted to Him as
Righteousness. Through the lineage of Abraham came Christ. The Angel Gabriel appeared to Mary and told her she would conceive by the power of the Holy Spirit and to name the baby "Jesus". Jesus was born in a manager in Bethlehem Ephratah (Micah 3:2)

His ministry of serving people was for 3 and ½ years. He was delivered to Pilate the Governor of Judaea on the Jewish Passover who ordered his crucifixion on a cross with 2 other malefactors. Jesus's last statement was "It is finished" (John 19:30).

The veil of the temple was rent in twain from the top to the bottom and there was a great earthquake, and the graves were opened and many bodies of the saints which slept arose and came out of the graves and went into the holy city and appeared unto many" (Matthew 27: 51-52). Nicodemus and Joseph of Arimathea requested the body of Jesus, from Pilate and were allowed to take his 'body' and place it in Joseph's new tomb. Roman guards were sent to prevent the body from being 'stolen' because he had said after 3 days he would rise again. Early in the morning on the third day there was a great earthquake for the angel of the Lord descended and rolled back the stone from the door and sat upon it and declared to the women who came, "He is risen as He said." The guards fell to the ground and then ran away and were paid to say that his body was stolen. John and Peter went into the tomb and found the burial cloth and the napkin folded on the slab where he lay. Jesus then appeared alive for 40 days, walking through walls, eating, showing the disciples his hands and his feet, appearing and then disappearing, until he was taken up into heaven and a cloud received him out of their sight (Acts 1:9).

The last command Jesus gave on earth was: "Go, ye therefore, and teach all nations, baptizing them in the name of the Father and of the Son and of the Holy Ghost: Teaching them to observe all things whatsoever I have commanded you and lo, I am with you always, *even* unto the end of the world. Amen. (Matthew 28:18-20).

BOOKS BY DAWN DENSMORE-PARENT:

"DIVINE ENCOUNTERS: The Reality of God, Angels, and Demons" Captivating accounts of God's extraordinary ways, including allowing individuals to appear after they die. Laugh as well as cry, as you see how God can use anything, even hippopotamuses to show His love.

"For Such a Time as This?" Mordecai asked Esther, "Who knoweth whether thou art come to the kingdom for such a time as this?" (Esther 4:14). My question is: "Are we, on earth now 'For Such a Time as This?

"Experiencing God's Amazing Ways" – Events that defy explanation. It truly is the power of God's Holy Spirit that allows us to experience the presence of the Lord – now!

"Experiencing God's Priceless, Precious Promises" Life's challenges offer us opportunities to be 'thankful' for all things in our life. For I know the thoughts that I think toward you, saith the Lord, thoughts of peace, and not of evil, to give you an expected end (Jeremiah 29;11)

"**The Truth Shall Set You Free: THE PRISON LETTERS**". This book contains 52 letters of extraordinary events and adventures of abundant living with Fabien.

"**The "True Man" Memory Book**" as told to Dawn Densmore-Parent, contains Trueman Bryer's memories from childhood, growing up, along with his marriage and amazing children. "But seek ye first the Kingdom of God and His Righteousness and all these things shall be added unto you" (Matthew 6:33)

"**The Incredible Life of a French Gypsy**" as told to Dawn Densmore-Parent contains memories of Claude D. "Frenchy" Mongeau, a French Gypsy, who traveled the world. His story of 'true love' warms the heart!

"**Still**" - contains events of Fabien Parent's recovery from a stroke, bladder cancer and a heart attack.

www.ingramcontent.com/pod-product-compliance
Lightning Source LLC
Chambersburg PA
CBHW042337040426
42446CB00021B/3478